White Fang

JACK LONDON

Level 2

Retold by Brigit Viney
Series Editors: Andy Hopkins and Jocelyn Potter

Pearson Education Limited
Edinburgh Gate, Harlow,
Essex CM20 2JE, England
and Associated Companies throughout the world.

ISBN 0 582 41815 1

First published 1905
This edition first published 2000

Second impression 2000

Text copyright © Penguin Books 2000
Illustrations copyright © Rob Hefferan (Advocate) 2000

Typeset by Digital Type, London
Set in 11/14pt Bembo
Printed in Spain by Mateu Cromo, S. A. Pinto (Madrid)

Published by Pearson Education Limited in association with
Penguin Books Ltd, both companies being subsidiaries of Pearson Plc

For a complete list of the titles available in the Penguin Readers series please write to your local
Pearson Education office or to: Marketing Department, Penguin Longman Publishing,
5 Bentinck Street, London W1M 5RN.

Contents

		page
Introduction		v
Chapter 1	The Gray Cub	1
Chapter 2	White Fang	4
Chapter 3	A Trip up the Mackenzie	9
Chapter 4	The Killer of Dogs	13
Chapter 5	The Great Fight	18
Chapter 6	Love Begins	22
Chapter 7	The Southland	27
Chapter 8	The God's Home	31
Chapter 9	Family Life	34
Activities		39

Introduction

He learned only about hate. Nobody gave him love, so he did not learn about that.

A young wolf, White Fang, is born near the Mackenzie River, in north-west Canada, in about 1893. One day he meets some Indians and they take him and his mother to their camp. They know his mother because she is half-dog. White Fang begins to learn the ways of men—and of other dogs. The dogs hate him, so he hates them. He learns to fight and to kill. It is a hard life, but will it change? Can White Fang learn to love?

When Jack London wrote *White Fang* in 1906, he was a famous writer. In 1903 his book *The Call of the Wild* (also a Penguin Reader) told the story of a dog, Buck. Buck has an easy life in sunny California, but then he goes to the Klondike in the cold north. Here he has to work, and to fight. American readers loved the story.

Wolves were very important to London. They were strong and wild, and they fought hard. He liked this in animals—and people.

Jack London was born in 1876 in San Francisco. His family had little money and he left school at fourteen. In the summer of 1897 he went to the Klondike. The trip was difficult and dangerous, and he had to stay there for the winter. He enjoyed the hard life and the strong people. Later, he wrote about the place in many of his books and stories.

After *White Fang*, London wrote thirty-two other books. He visited Australia, and had a farm in California. He died in 1916.

Chapter 1   The Gray Cub

The two wolves moved slowly down the Mackenzie River. Often they left it and looked for food by the smaller rivers. But they always went back to the large river.

The she-wolf looked everywhere for a home, and then one day she found it. It was a cave near a small river. She looked inside it very carefully. It was warm and dry so she lay down.

The he-wolf was hungry. He lay down inside the cave but he did not sleep well. He could hear the sound of water and he could see the April sun on the snow. Under the snow, and in the trees, there was new life.

The he-wolf left the cave and followed the ice bed of the small river. He wanted food. But eight hours later he came back, hungrier than before. In the wet snow he was slow and could not catch anything.

Strange sounds came from inside the cave. When he looked inside, the she-wolf snarled at him. He moved away and slept at the mouth of the cave.

The next morning he saw five strange little animals next to the she-wolf. They made weak little noises but their eyes were not open. He left the cave quickly. He had to find food for the she-wolf. This time, when he took meat back to her, she did not snarl at him.

Four of the cubs were red, but one was gray. This gray cub was a fighter. He fought his brothers and sisters more than they fought him. He always wanted to leave the cave and his mother had to stop him.

Then, after a time, there was no food. His father did not bring them any meat, and his mother had no milk. The cubs cried, but then they slept.

When the gray cub felt strong again, he only had one sister. The other cubs were dead. His sister slept all the time. Then the fire of life in her died too.

Later, the cub's father died. The she-wolf knew this because she found his body in the woods. Near his dead body lived a large wildcat. The she-wolf found the wildcat's cave, but she did not go inside it. The wildcat was in there, with her babies, and she was dangerous.

One day, the cub left the cave and began to walk. He hurt his feet and he ran into things. He often fell, but he learned quickly.

In the woods he found a very young, thin, yellow animal. He turned it over with his foot and it made a strange noise. Suddenly, its mother jumped on him and bit his neck. Then she took her baby into the trees.

The cub sat down and made weak little noises. He was there when the mother animal came back. He saw her long thin body and long thin head. She came nearer and nearer and then she bit his neck again. He snarled and tried to fight. But the mother animal fought hard. She wanted to kill him.

Suddenly, the she-wolf ran through the trees and caught the mother animal between her teeth. Her mouth closed on the long yellow body. Then she and the cub ate the animal.

After that, the cub went out every day and killed for food. Then one day the she-wolf brought home a baby wildcat. The cub ate it and fell asleep in the cave next to his mother.

He woke when she snarled loudly. The mother wildcat was at the mouth of the cave. She snarled angrily and the hair on the cub's back stood up. Because the mouth of the cave was small, the wildcat had to come in on her stomach. She and the she-wolf fought hard. The cub fought too and bit the wildcat's leg. She hit him hard but he did not stop fighting.

In the end, he and his mother killed the wildcat. But after the

The mother wildcat was at the mouth of the cave.

fight his mother was very weak and sick. For a day and a night she did not move. For a week she only left the cave for water. But at the end of the week she could look for meat again.

For some time the cub could not walk very well, but then he began to look for meat with his mother. He was not afraid of small animals now. He could fight with his mother and kill a large animal.

He liked killing other animals. He also liked eating, running, fighting, and sleeping. He liked the life in his body. He was happy in his world.

Chapter 2   White Fang

The cub ran to the small river. He was heavy with sleep and he wanted to drink. He did not look around him carefully.

Suddenly, he saw them under the trees. Five big animals sat in front of him. They did not snarl or show their teeth. They looked at him and did not move. They were dangerous, but the gray cub could not move. He felt very weak and small next to them.

One of them got up and came to him. When he put his hand near the cub, the cub's hair stood up. He showed his little fangs. The man laughed and said: "*Wabam wabisca ip pit tah.*" ("Look! The white fangs!")

The other men laughed loudly. The first man put his hand near the cub again. This time the cub bit it. The man hit him on the head. The cub fell and then cried. The men laughed again.

Then the cub heard something. The Indians heard it too.

The cub's mother ran to him and snarled loudly at the men.

"Kiche!" said one of the men. "Kiche!"

The cub's mother stopped snarling and lay down on the

"Look! The white fangs!"

ground. Why? The cub did not understand. His mother fought everything!

The man came to her. He put his hand on her head, but she did not bite him! The other men put their hands on her head and she did not bite them. The men made noises with their mouths.

"It is not strange," one man said. "Her father was a wolf and her mother was a dog."

"She ran away last year, Gray Beaver. Do you remember?" said a second man.

"Yes. She ran to the wolves because we could find no meat for the dogs."

He put his hand on the cub. The cub snarled and the hand quickly hit him. The cub closed his mouth. Then the man stroked the cub's back and behind his ears.

"His father is a wolf," said the man. "His fangs are white, so his name will be White Fang. He is my dog because Kiche was my dead brother's dog."

The men made more mouth noises. Then Gray Beaver cut some wood from a tree. He tied Kiche to it with some leather. Then he tied the stick to a small tree.

After a time, about forty men, women, and children and many dogs came through the trees. The people and dogs carried heavy bags. A small boy took Kiche's stick and walked away with her. White Fang followed her.

They walked by the small river for a time. Then they came to the large Mackenzie River and the Indians made their camp next to it.

White Fang walked around the camp and looked at everything. A young dog walked slowly to him. This dog, Lip-lip, did not like other dogs, and he bit White Fang badly. White Fang fought him angrily, but Lip-lip was older and stronger. He bit

White Fang again and again, so White Fang ran back to his mother. This was the first of many fights with Lip-lip.

Five minutes later, White Fang left Kiche and looked around the camp again. He saw Gray Beaver and went to him. Gray Beaver sat on the ground near a lot of sticks. Women and children brought Gray Beaver more sticks. Then a strange thing came up from the sticks on the ground. It was the color of the sun. White Fang went near it, and suddenly his nose hurt. He jumped away fast and cried. Gray Beaver and the others laughed loudly.

White Fang ran back to his mother and lay down next to her. His nose hurt and he wanted to go back to the woods. He watched the men in the camp. They were large and strong, and they made fire! They were gods to him.

One of the Indians, Three Eagles, planned a trip up the Mackenzie River. Before he left, Gray Beaver gave him Kiche. So one morning, Three Eagles took Kiche onto his boat. The boat started to move up the river. White Fang jumped into the water and swam after it. He did not listen to the angry shouts of Gray Beaver. He wanted his mother.

Gray Beaver followed him in his boat. He caught White Fang's neck and pulled him angrily out of the water. He hit him hard, again and again. White Fang snarled at him angrily. Gray Beaver hit him faster and harder. Then White Fang felt very afraid. He stopped snarling.

Gray Beaver stopped hitting him. He threw him into the bottom of the boat and kicked him hard. White Fang suddenly felt angry again and bit Gray Beaver's foot.

This time Gray Beaver was really angry. He hit White Fang very hard for a long time. Again, he threw him to the bottom of the boat and again he kicked him angrily. This time White Fang did not bite him.

He caught White Fang's neck and pulled him angrily out of the water.

Later, in the night, White Fang remembered his mother and felt sad. He cried loudly, and Gray Beaver hit him again. After that he only cried quietly when the gods were near. But sometimes in the woods he cried loudly again. He stayed in the camp and waited for his mother.

He was not too sad. Life in the camp was interesting because the gods did many strange things. But the young dog Lip-lip hated him and often started fights with him. The other young dogs followed Lip-lip and started fights with White Fang too.

These fights taught him some important lessons. He learned to stay on his feet in a fight. He also learned to hurt a dog very badly in a very short time. He learned to push the dog off his feet and to bite his neck. He learned these lessons because he wanted to live. He had to be faster, more intelligent, and more dangerous than the other dogs.

One day, he killed a dog in a fight. The Indians saw him and were angry with him. After that, they did not want him near them. They shouted at him angrily when they saw him.

This life turned White Fang into a very angry, dangerous animal. He learned only about hate. Nobody gave him any love, so he did not learn about that.

Chapter 3   A Trip up the Mackenzie

In the fall the Indians put everything from the camp into bags. Then they put the bags into their boats. Some of the boats left and White Fang understood.

He ran out of the camp and through a small river. Then he found a place in the woods and went to sleep. He woke when he heard Gray Beaver. Gray Beaver called his name again and again. Then he stopped calling and went back to the camp.

White Fang played in the woods for a time, but then he suddenly felt afraid. The woods were dark and cold, and the trees made loud noises. He ran back to the camp, but there was nobody there. He sat down and looked up at the sky. He cried sadly to the large night sky.

In the morning he began to run by the river. All day he ran. Sometimes he had to climb high mountains behind the river. Sometimes he had to swim across other, smaller rivers. He always followed the large river on its way. All the time he looked for the gods.

He ran all night and the next day. He felt weak and hungry and his feet hurt badly. Snow began to fall and he could not find his way easily. Then night fell and the snow came down more heavily.

Then he smelled the gods through the snow on the ground. He left the river and went into the trees. He heard the sounds of the gods and saw Gray Beaver near a fire.

He felt afraid but he walked slowly into the firelight. Gray Beaver saw him and looked at him. White Fang went to him and waited. But Gray Beaver did not hit him. He gave him some meat! White Fang carefully smelled it and then ate it. He sat at Gray Beaver's feet and looked at the fire. He felt warm and happy. This was his place.

Some months later, in the middle of December, Gray Beaver went up the Mackenzie River. His son Mit-sah and his wife Kloo-klooch went with him. They took two sleds. Mit-sah's sled was smaller and lighter than Gray Beaver's, but it carried a lot of food.

Gray Beaver and Mit-sah tied White Fang and six other dogs to Mit-sah's sled. Lip-lip ran at the front. All day the other dogs ran behind him. They wanted to catch him, but they could not. Because of this they hated him. In the camp Lip-lip had to stay

He felt afraid but he walked slowly into the firelight.

near the gods because the other dogs hated him. He was not the most important dog now.

At one village, White Fang learned something new. One day a boy cut some meat and some of it fell on the ground. White Fang ate it. The boy ran after him and tried to hit him with a heavy stick. White Fang was very angry. He bit the boy's hand hard. The boy's family came to Gray Beaver but he spoke angrily to them. He did not hit White Fang.

Later that day, some boys from the village began to hit Mit-sah in the woods. White Fang ran angrily to them and they ran away. When Mit-sah told this story in the camp, Gray Beaver gave White Fang a lot of meat. White Fang understood. There were different gods. There were his gods, and there were other gods. His gods were the most important.

They arrived in Gray Beaver's village in April. White Fang was now a year old. He was tall and thin, and his coat was wolf-gray. He walked through the village and saw the gods and dogs from the summer. He was not afraid of the older dogs. He could fight them and win.

In the summer, he saw Kiche outside the village. He stopped and looked at her. He remembered her, but she did not remember him. He ran to her happily, but she bit him in the face. He ran away from her. He did not understand.

Kiche now had new cubs, so she could not remember her older ones. One of her new cubs came to White Fang. White Fang smelled him and Kiche jumped on him angrily. She bit his face a second time. Then White Fang left. This was a she-wolf and he could not fight her.

In the third year of White Fang's life, there was no food on the Mackenzie for a long time. In the summer, the Indians could not find any fish and in the winter they could not find any wild animals. They ate their leather shoes, and the dogs. The old and weak gods died and the other gods cried all the time. Some of the most intelligent dogs understood, and they went into the woods for food. There, the wolves ate them.

White Fang also went into the woods. For months he was very hungry, but he always killed something. Other animals wanted to kill him, but he could run faster than them.

Early in the summer, he met Lip-lip in the woods. He was not hungry, but he snarled at Lip-lip. He pushed him to the ground and bit his neck hard. That was the end of Lip-lip.

One day, White Fang came to the end of the woods. In front of him he saw the Mackenzie and a village. It was the old village, but it was now in a new place.

He left the woods and went to the village. Gray Beaver was not there, but **Kloo-kooh** gave him a fish. He felt happy because he was with the gods again.

Chapter 4   The Killer of Dogs

When White Fang was almost five years old, Gray Beaver took him on a second trip. This time they went down the Mackenzie, across the mountains and down the Porcupine River to the Yukon River. They stopped in many villages, and in each village White Fang fought the dogs. The dogs often died because they fought in a different way from White Fang.

White Fang liked fighting very quickly. He hated being very near another animal because it felt dangerous. He had to feel free, so he finished his fights very fast. Usually, he won his fights because the village dogs were slower. Sometimes a dog hurt him badly, but these times were accidents. Usually, he was too fast for them.

In the summer, Gray Beaver and White Fang arrived at Fort

Yukon. It was 1898, and there were thousands of people in the town. These people planned to go up the Yukon to the Klondike because they wanted to find gold.

In Fort Yukon, White Fang saw white gods for the first time. A small number of them lived in the town, and other men came from the boats. These boats stopped in the town two or three times a week.

He was very afraid of the white gods because they were stronger than the Indians. But he was not afraid of their dogs. They did not fight well. When they ran at him, he jumped away. Then he pushed them to the ground and bit them in the neck. It was easy.

Sometimes a dog did not get up after a fight with White Fang. Then White Fang left him to the Indian dogs. They jumped on him and killed him. White Fang never killed a white god's dog. He was too intelligent. The white gods were always angry when their dogs died in a fight. They hit the Indian dogs hard with sticks.

White Fang started these fights easily. When the strange dogs left the boat, he went to them. They were afraid of him because he was wild. He was dangerous to them and to their gods so they wanted to fight him.

After two or three of these fights, the white gods always took their dogs back to their boat. That was the end of the game with the dogs from that boat.

After a time, these fights were the only thing in White Fang's life. Gray Beaver had no work for him because he was too busy. He sold leather shoes to the white gods and he was now rich.

White Fang liked the fights, but he was not happy. He did not love an animal or a god, because no animal or god loved him. Everybody hated him.

The white men in Fort Yukon did not like the white men

They were afraid of him because he was wild.

from the boats. These men were from the south, and were weak. The men from Fort Yukon liked the dog fights because the weak men's dogs died.

One man liked the fights more than the other men. He watched each fight. Sometimes when a Southland dog died, he shouted happily. He wanted very much to buy White Fang.

This man's name was Beauty Smith. His name was "Beauty" because he was very ugly and small. He had large yellow teeth and dirty yellow eyes. The thin hair on his head and face was also dirty yellow.

He tried to make friends with White Fang but White Fang hated him. He always showed his teeth to him and moved away.

Then Beauty Smith visited Gray Beaver in his camp. Beauty Smith and Gray Beaver talked for a long time. Gray Beaver did not want to sell White Fang. White Fang was his strongest dog. But Beauty Smith knew Gray Beaver. He visited him often. Each time he took a black bottle with him, under his coat. Gray Beaver began to want more and more bottles. In a short time all his money went on them. Then Beauty Smith talked to him again about White Fang. He wanted to pay for White Fang in bottles, not dollars. This time Gray Beaver listened.

"You catch him, you take him," he said.

After two days, Beauty Smith told Gray Beaver, "*You* catch him."

That evening, White Fang came quietly into the camp. The bad white god was not there. Gray Beaver came over to him and tied some leather round his neck. He sat down next to White Fang and drank from his bottle.

After an hour, Beauty Smith walked into the camp. He stood over White Fang. White Fang snarled up at him. A hand moved down to his head. Suddenly, White Fang tried to bite it. The hand jumped back. Gray Beaver hit White Fang on the head.

Beauty Smith went away and came back with a large stick.

Beauty Smith came back with a large stick.

Gray Beaver gave him the leather and Beauty Smith walked away from White Fang. The leather pulled at White Fang's neck but he did not move. Then he suddenly jumped at the bad god. Beauty Smith did not move away. He hit White Fang hard with his stick. White Fang fell to the ground. Beauty Smith pulled the leather again, and this time White Fang followed him.

In the town, Beauty Smith tied him with the leather and went to bed. White Fang waited an hour. Then he began to bite the leather. When he was free he went back to Gray Beaver.

In the morning, Gray Beaver gave him to Beauty Smith again. Beauty Smith hit him very hard with the stick. He enjoyed hurting him.

Then he took White Fang to the town again. This time he tied him with a stick. In the night, White Fang began to bite the stick. After many hours, he bit through it and was free. He went back to Gray Beaver. He could not leave him.

Beauty Smith came for him again the next morning. He hit him harder than before. When he finished, White Fang was very sick. He could not see and he could not walk easily. He followed Beauty Smith back to the town.

Gray Beaver said nothing to Beauty Smith because White Fang was not his dog now. After a short time, he left Fort Yukon for the Mackenzie.

Chapter 5   The Great Fight

When the first snows began to fall, Beauty Smith took White Fang on a boat up the Yukon to Dawson. He called White Fang "The Killer Wolf" and showed him to people for money. When White Fang slept, people woke him with a stick. They wanted to see an angry wolf.

White Fang was very angry. He hated everything and everybody. He hated Beauty Smith because he hurt him all the time. Beauty Smith wanted an angry wolf because he wanted a fighter.

Sometimes, at night, Beauty Smith took White Fang into the woods outside the town. In the morning, a lot of people and a dog arrived. White Fang fought the dog. Usually, he killed him. He was a better fighter than the other dogs.

After a time, the fights stopped because Beauty Smith could not find dogs for them. Then, in the spring, he suddenly took him to a fight. It was a fight with a very strange dog.

This dog was short and heavy. The people shouted to him, "Go to him, Cherokee! Eat him!"

But Cherokee did not really want to fight. Then a man began to stroke the dog's body from its bottom to its head. Suddenly, Cherokee felt angry and he began to run to White Fang.

White Fang quickly jumped on him and bit him behind his ear. The dog did not snarl. He turned and followed White Fang. Again and again White Fang jumped on Cherokee and bit him. Again and again Cherokee followed him. He planned to do something, but what? White Fang could not understand him. And he could not bite his neck below his head. Cherokee was too short, and his head was too large.

Again and again White Fang tried to push Cherokee onto the ground, but Cherokee was too short and heavy. Then White Fang pushed too hard and fell to the ground. Cherokee bit into his neck. White Fang jumped up and ran. Cherokee's teeth stayed in his neck. White Fang hated this. He hated being near the other dog. He ran around and around.

He only stopped when he was tired. Cherokee pushed him onto his back and sat on top of him. His teeth did not leave

White Fang's neck. Slowly, he moved his teeth up White Fang's neck. Beauty Smith began to kick White Fang angrily.

Suddenly, a tall young man pushed his way through the people to Beauty Smith. He was very angry and his gray eyes were cold. He hit Beauty Smith in the face. Beauty Smith fell to the ground.

"Matt, come here," the young man called.

A shorter, older man went to him and they tried to pull Cherokee off White Fang.

"You can't pull him off, Scott," said Matt. "We have to open his mouth."

Scott took out his gun and pushed it between Cherokee's teeth. Then he slowly opened the dog's mouth and Matt pulled White Fang's neck out from the dog's teeth.

White Fang tried to get up, but his legs were too weak. He fell back into the snow.

Beauty Smith got up slowly and came to him. He looked at him.

"Matt, how much does a good sled-dog cost?" Scott asked.

"Three hundred dollars."

"And how much for this dog now?"

"Half of that."

Scott turned to Beauty Smith.

"Did you hear that? I'm going to take your dog, and I'm going to give you a hundred and fifty dollars for him."

He took out the money.

"I'm not selling," said Beauty Smith.

"Oh yes, you are," said Scott. "Because I'm buying. Here's your money."

Beauty Smith put his hands behind him and moved away. Scott ran after him.

"Take the money or I'll hit you again," he said.

Matt pulled White Fang's neck out from the dog's teeth.

"All right," Beauty Smith said quickly. "But I'm going to tell the police in Dawson."

"Then you'll have to leave town. Do you understand?"

"Yes," answered Beauty Smith and moved away.

Scott turned his back on him and went to White Fang.

Chapter 6   Love Begins

Weedon Scott sat outside his small house in the woods and looked at White Fang. White Fang snarled angrily at Matt's sled dogs.

"He's a wolf, and we can't change him," Scott said to Matt.

"Wolf or dog, he can pull a sled," said Matt. "Look at these lines on his back."

"Can he be a sled-dog again?" Scott asked. He was interested in this idea.

"Maybe. Let's see. Untie him."

Scott looked at him.

"*You* untie him!" he said.

So Matt took a heavy stick and went to White Fang. He untied him. White Fang slowly walked away from him. He could not understand these gods. They did not hit him.

Scott went into the house and came out with some meat. He threw it to White Fang. White Fang jumped away from it and looked at it.

One of Matt's dogs jumped for the meat. Then White Fang jumped on him and bit him. The dog fell to the ground. Matt ran to him, but he was too late. The dog quickly died.

"We'll have to kill him," Scott said.

"Don't kill him now, Mr. Scott," Matt answered. "Maybe he'll change."

"I don't want to kill him," Scott said. "I want to be nice to him."

He walked to White Fang and started to talk to him quietly. He moved his hand near White Fang. Suddenly, White Fang bit it. Scott cried out and White Fang moved away.

Matt ran into the house and came out with a gun. White Fang began to snarl loudly at him.

"Don't kill him! He knows that guns are dangerous!" Scott said. "He's very intelligent."

"All right," Matt said. He put the gun down and White Fang stopped snarling.

"You're right, Mr. Scott. He knows that a gun can kill," he said.

The next day, Scott sat outside the house. White Fang watched him. Scott began to speak. White Fang snarled, but Scott did not move. He spoke quietly for a long time. White Fang stopped snarling and listened to the sound of the god.

After a long time, the god got up and went into the house. When he came out, he sat down in the same place. He had some meat in his hand. White Fang's ears stood up and he looked at the meat. It was good meat, but he did not go near it. He was afraid of the god.

Then the god threw the meat on the snow at White Fang's feet. He smelled it carefully but he did not look at it. He watched the god. Nothing happened. The god did not get up, and he did not hit him. White Fang took the meat and ate it.

The god showed him some more meat in his hand, and again White Fang did not go to him. Again the god threw it to him in the snow. The god repeated this a number of times. But then he did not throw the meat to him. He only showed it to him in his hand. The meat was good, and White Fang was hungry. Slowly, he went near the hand and then he took the meat from it. His eyes never left the god's face, and the hair on his neck stood up. He ate the meat, but nothing happened.

Slowly, he went near the hand and then he took the meat from it.

He waited. The god talked again, quietly and warmly. Then he put his hand lightly on White Fang's head. White Fang felt very afraid, but he also felt happy. He hated the hand, but he liked the warm sound of the words. He snarled, but he did not bite the hand. The god stroked White Fang's head lightly again and again. White Fang began to like it.

In this way, White Fang's old life ended, and his new life began. Slowly, he learned new lessons and forgot old ones. He did not run away, because he liked this god. Then he began to really love him. Without him, he was very sad.

In the early morning, he did not run in the woods, but waited for the man outside the house for hours. At night, when the man came home, White Fang left his warm place under the snow. He wanted to see and hear the god. He wanted to be with him. White Fang did not show his love openly. He never ran to the god. Only his eyes showed his love.

In the late spring, the man suddenly went away. White Fang waited all night for him outside the house, but he did not come. Days came and went. The man did not come back. White Fang was sick for the first time in his life. Matt brought him inside the house. He wrote to Scott:

"The wolf can't work or eat. He wants you. He's going to die without you."

Then, one evening, White Fang suddenly made a quiet noise and got up. His ears stood up and he listened hard. The door opened and Weedon Scott came in. He spoke to Matt and then looked around the room.

"Where's the wolf?" he asked.

Then he saw him near the fire. He called him and White Fang came to him quickly. A strange light shone in his eyes.

"He never looked at *me* that way," said Matt.

Scott did not hear him. He was face to face with White Fang.

He stroked him, again and again, behind his ears, on his back.

He stroked him, again and again, behind his ears, on his back. White Fang felt a very strong love for him and suddenly he pushed his head between Scott's arm and body. It stayed there for a long time.

Scott looked at Matt. His eyes shone.

"I knew it! This wolf is a dog. Look at him!" said Matt.

White Fang felt better because he was happy again. A day later he left the house and went outside. The sled-dogs jumped on him and he fought them happily. He was well and strong and there was life in him again!

Chapter 7   The Southland

"Listen to that!" said Matt at dinner one night.

Through the door came a quiet, sad noise.

"That wolf knows that you're leaving," said Matt.

"What can I do with a wolf in California?" asked Scott.

A second sad noise came through the door.

"How does he know that you're going?" asked Matt.

"I don't know," answered Scott, sadly.

One morning, White Fang saw Scott's open bags on the floor of the house. Scott and Matt came and went all day. Sometimes Scott put things in the bags. White Fang could not eat. That night he cried loudly outside the house. The next day he felt very afraid. He followed Scott everywhere.

Two Indians arrived and took Scott's bags. Scott came to the door of the house and called White Fang inside. He stroked White Fang behind his ears and spoke to him sadly.

"I'm sorry," he said. "I'm going a long way, and you can't come with me."

White Fang pushed his head between Scott's arm and body.

From the river came the sound of a boat. Matt and Scott got up and left the house quickly. They shut the front door and the back door, and they went down to the river.

"Be good to him, Matt," said Scott. "Write and tell me about him."

"I will," said Matt. "Listen to him!"

White Fang cried loudly in the house behind them.

On the boat the two men said goodbye. Suddenly, Matt saw White Fang! He was on the boat!

The two men went to him and they found cuts on his face and body.

"We forgot the window. He jumped through it!" said Matt.

Scott thought quickly.

"Goodbye, Matt, old man. About the wolf—don't write. I—"

"What! You mean—?"

"Yes! *I'll* write to *you* about him!"

Later, when White Fang arrived in San Francisco, he felt very afraid. There were a lot of people, and he could not look at them. The noise in the streets hurt his ears and the houses were very large. He stayed near his god all the time.

The god took him to a small room and left him there for a long time. The room was full of bags. When the god came back, they left the city. They were in quiet country now.

A man and a woman came to his god, and the woman put her arms around his neck. She wanted to fight him! White Fang jumped at her and snarled angrily. His god stopped him.

"It's all right, Mother," Scott said. "He'll learn."

The woman laughed, but her face was white. She was afraid.

Scott spoke quietly to White Fang, and then more loudly: "Down! Down!"

White Fang lay down.

Scott put his arms around his mother, and watched White Fang.

White Fang jumped at her and snarled angrily.

"Down!" he repeated.

White Fang watched them. This time he did not jump up at the woman.

The gods got into a carriage and drove away. White Fang ran behind them. After fifteen minutes the carriage turned into a small road between two lines of trees.

Suddenly, a dog stood between White Fang and the carriage. Its eyes shone angrily. White Fang ran to it but stopped. He could not fight it because it was a she-dog. She was afraid of him so she jumped at him. She bit him, but he did not hurt her. He tried to move around her but she stopped him.

"Here, Collie!" called the strange god in the carriage.

Weedon Scott laughed.

"It's all right, Father. White Fang will have to learn many things. He can start learning now."

The carriage drove away, but Collie did not move. White Fang ran around her and she followed quickly. Suddenly, he turned and pushed her to the ground. Then he ran after the carriage. She followed but she could not catch him.

The carriage stopped at a large house. When White Fang came to the house, a large dog suddenly ran to him very fast. It pushed him to the ground. White Fang jumped up and almost bit the dog's neck. But then Collie angrily jumped on him. Again White Fang fell to the ground.

His god came and stroked White Fang. Another god called the other dogs to him. Under his god's hand White Fang felt better.

The carriage left and more strange gods came out of the house. Two of them put their arms around his god's neck, but White Fang did not move.

The gods walked into the house. White Fang followed Scott.

"Take Collie inside and leave Dick and your dog outside. They'll fight and then they'll be friends," said Scott's father.

"Dick'll be dead in two minutes!" answered Scott. "The wolf will have to come inside."

Chapter 8   The God's Home

White Fang learned quickly about life at Sierra Vista, Scott's home. He was not friendly with the other dogs, but he did not fight them. Dick wanted to be friends, but White Fang always snarled at him. In the end, Dick did not come near him. Collie always wanted to fight him because he was a wolf. When White Fang saw her, he turned away. When she bit him, he walked away slowly and carefully.

He learned about his god's family. There was his mother, his father, his wife, his two sisters, and his two children, Weedon and Maud. White Fang did not like children, because they always hurt him. But these children were very important to his god, so he did not snarl at them. After a time, he began to like them. He did not go to them, but he waited for them. When they left him, he was sad.

After the children, White Fang liked his god's father best. When he read the newspaper, White Fang sat at his feet. Sometimes Scott's father looked at him and said something. But White Fang only sat with him when his god was not there. When *his* god was there, White Fang was not interested in the other gods. He never looked at them with love, and he never put his head between their arm and body. He only did this with his god.

One morning, White Fang found a chicken outside the chicken house. He killed it and ate it. It was fat and good, and White Fang wanted more.

Later in the day, he saw a second chicken outside the chicken house. This time a man ran and hit White Fang with some leather. At the first cut of the leather, White Fang left the chicken for the man. He jumped for his neck. The man put his arm over his neck and White Fang bit his arm.

Suddenly, Collie jumped on White Fang. She was very angry. She ran around him again and again and in the end White Fang ran away from her.

"He'll learn about the chickens," Scott told his father, "but I'll have to catch him with them."

Two nights later, White Fang climbed into one of the chicken houses. He killed every chicken in it.

In the morning, Scott found him. He put White Fang's nose next to the dead chickens and spoke to him angrily. He hit him lightly on the neck. Then he took him inside another chicken house. White Fang wanted to kill the chickens, but the god's words stopped him. He did not kill chickens again.

In this way, Scott taught White Fang about life at Sierra Vista. Sometimes Scott hit him lightly. This hurt White Fang very much because of his great love. When Gray Beaver and Beauty Smith hit him, he felt angry. But when Scott hit him he felt very sad. Usually, Scott did not hit him. He spoke to him, and White Fang understood.

White Fang learned about life in the town too. There was meat in the stores, but he could not eat it. There were cats in some of the houses, and dogs everywhere, but he could not fight them. There were people everywhere, and they often wanted to stroke him. He did not snarl at them. It was not easy, but he learned the ways of the Southland.

On the way to town, three dogs always jumped on him when they saw him. Each time some men in the street shouted at the four dogs because they wanted to watch a fight.

He put White Fang's nose next to the dead chickens and spoke to him angrily.

One day, they shouted at the dogs and the god stopped the carriage.

"Go to them," he said to White Fang.

White Fang looked at him.

"Go to them," he repeated. "Eat them."

White Fang did not wait. He jumped on the dogs, and quickly killed them all.

After that the dogs in the town did not jump on him.

Chapter 9   Family Life

The months came and went. There was a lot of food and no work in the Southland, so White Fang was fatter than in the Northland. Life was not dangerous, and White Fang was not afraid of anything.

The only problem in White Fang's life was Collie. She snarled at him all the time and followed him around the farm. She could not forget the dead chickens. When he looked at a chicken, she was very angry. Then White Fang lay down and closed his eyes. She went away when he did this.

The gods were good to him, so he was happy. Sometimes his god laughed at him. White Fang could not be angry with his god, but he had to do something. He tried not to move his face, but his god laughed harder. In the end, White Fang's mouth opened and his eyes shone with love. He laughed!

He also played with his god. They fought in a friendly way. He snarled at his god, but he never bit him. At the end of the game, the god always put his arms around White Fang's neck.

The god often went out on his horse and White Fang went with him. One day, his god fell from the horse and could not get up. White Fang jumped angrily at the horse's neck, but his god stopped him.

"Home! Go home!" he said.

White Fang did not want to leave him. He walked away, but then came back. Scott talked to him quietly and White Fang listened carefully.

"Go home and tell them, wolf. Go home!" he repeated.

White Fang understood "home" so he ran back to the house. The children ran to him, but he pushed past them. He turned to his god's wife and took her dress in his teeth. He snarled and snarled.

"I hope he isn't going crazy," said Scott's mother. "Maybe it's too hot for him here."

"He's trying to speak, I think," said Beth, Scott's sister.

White Fang snarled again.

They all stood up and followed him to Scott.

After this, Scott's family loved him more.

In the second winter in the Southland, Collie changed. When she bit him, her teeth did not really hurt. She sometimes wanted to play with him.

One day she ran into the woods. White Fang's god was on his horse. He wanted to leave the farm with White Fang. But White Fang had to follow Collie. He ran with her through the woods for a long way.

One night after this, White Fang woke suddenly. He was inside the house, near the front door. He smelled a strange god and heard a strange sound. He made no noise, but got up. He followed the strange god to the bottom of the stairs. The stranger began to climb the stairs. At the top of the stairs was the bedroom of White Fang's god.

White Fang did not snarl—he quietly jumped on the man's back and bit him. They fell to the floor. White Fang jumped at him again and bit him again.

Tables, chairs, and glass fell and broke. The noise woke the

But then he closed his eyes and went to sleep in the sun.

family. There were the sounds of a gun and a man's loud shouts. Then the noise stopped.

Weedon and his father came down the stairs. A dead man was on the floor, under the chairs and tables.

They turned to White Fang. He was on the floor too. Scott's father called the doctor.

The doctor worked for an hour and a half on White Fang.

"He's very sick," said the doctor. "I think he's going to die."

But White Fang was strong and did not die. He slept and slept. In his sleep he lived again the days with his mother, Gray Beaver, and Beauty Smith.

Then one day he got up. It was difficult, but he stood up. The gods watched him.

"Take him outside," said the doctor. "He has to walk."

They all followed White Fang outside. He felt very weak. He had to lie down outside the house for a long time. But then he began to walk again, and he started to feel stronger.

At the farm he saw Collie. Next to her were six fat little dogs. She snarled, so he did not go near them.

His god pushed one little dog next to him. Collie snarled again. White Fang was interested in the little dog and watched him. He put his nose next to the little dog's nose and washed its face.

Then he felt weak again and lay down. The other little dogs ran to him and climbed over him. Their bodies felt strange. But then he closed his eyes and went to sleep in the sun.

ACTIVITIES

Chapters 1–3

Before you read

1 The words in *italics* are all in the story. Find them in your dictionary.

    a Look at the pictures on pages 3 and 5. Find these animals and things in them.

       cave   cub   fangs   wolf

    b Put these words in the table.

       bite   lie down   smell   snarl   stroke   tie

People do this	Animals do this

    c Answer the questions.

       Where does *leather* come from?

       What does a *sled* move on?

       What can you do with a *stick*?

       What, in your *body*, do you use when you eat?

    d Put these words in the sentences.

       camp   god   neck   village

       My ..... hurts, so I can't turn my head.

       Our family lived in this ..... for twenty years.

       They made a ..... for the night near the river.

       People killed animals because they wanted the rain ..... to bring rain.

2 White Fang is a wolf. What do you know about wolves?

After you read

3 These chapters tell the story of the first three years in White Fang's life. What can he do at the end of them?

4 Is White Fang's life better with or without the Indians? Why? What do you think?

Chapters 4–6

Before you read

5 Look at the names of Chapters 4–6. What is going to happen to White Fang, do you think?

6 Where do you find *gold*? Find the word in your dictionary. Why did a lot of North Americans look for it in the 1890s?

After you read

7 Why does White Fang lose the fight with Cherokee?

8 Work with another student.

Student A: You are Beauty Smith. You visit Weedon Scott and you ask for White Fang back. Why do you want him?

Student B: You are Weedon Scott. Answer Beauty Smith.

Chapters 7–9

Before you read

9 Chapter 7 is about the "Southland." Where do you think this is? How will it be different for White Fang? What will he do there?

10 Find the word *carriage* in your dictionary. What pulls a carriage?

After you read

11 Talk to two other students.

Students A
and B: You are Scott's mother and father. Scott is in the South again. Ask him about White Fang. How will he live in your house?

Student C: You are Scott. Answer their questions.

12 How does White Fang help

a Weedon Scott? **b** the Scott family?

Writing

13 Write about the fight between White Fang and Cherokee for a newspaper.

14 You are somebody in Weedon Scott's family. Write a letter to a friend a week after Weedon comes back. Tell them about White Fang.

15 White Fang is sick. You are Weedon Scott. Write a letter to Matt. Tell him about life at Sierra Vista with White Fang.

16 It is a year later. What is White Fang doing now, do you think? Write about a day in his life.

Answers for the Activities in this book are published in our free resource packs for teachers, the Penguin Readers Factsheets, or available on a separate sheet. Please write to your local Pearson Education office or to: Marketing Department, Penguin Longman Publishing, 5 Bentinck Street, London W1M 5RN.